NORWAY

NORWAY 2016 HUMAN RIGHTS REPORT

EXECUTIVE SUMMARY

Norway is a parliamentary democracy and constitutional monarchy. The government consists of a prime minister, a cabinet, and a 169-seat parliament (Storting), which is elected every four years and may not be dissolved. The monarch generally appoints the leader of the majority party or majority coalition as prime minister with the approval of parliament. Observers considered the multiparty parliamentary elections in 2013 to be free and fair.

Civilian authorities maintained effective control over the security forces.

The most significant human rights problems included violence against women and children, which was a continuing societal problem. Asylum seekers were restricted in their movement and could not work. Hate speech on the internet targeted ethnic and religious minorities, and lesbian, gay, bisexual, transgender, and intersex (LGBTI) persons.

Other problems included the use in some cases of solitary confinement to hold detainees before trial longer than the 48 hours permitted by law. Nongovernmental organizations (NGOs) reported anti-Muslim and anti-Arab sentiment in society and discrimination against immigrants remained a problem. Women were subject to discrimination in employment. There were some reports of social and employment discrimination based on religious affiliation, belief, or practice. Incidents of forced and child labor were reported.

The government investigated officials who committed violations, whether in the security forces or elsewhere in the government.

Section 1. Respect for the Integrity of the Person, Including Freedom from:

a. Arbitrary Deprivation of Life and other Unlawful or Politically Motivated Killings

There were no reports that the government or its agents committed arbitrary or unlawful killings.

b. Disappearance

There were no reports of politically motivated disappearances.

c. Torture and Other Cruel, Inhuman, or Degrading Treatment or Punishment

The constitution and law prohibit such practices, and there were no reports that government officials employed them.

Prison and Detention Center Conditions

There were no significant reports regarding prison or detention center conditions that raised human rights concerns.

Physical Conditions: In April a court ruled that a convicted murderer was subject to prison conditions that violated the European Convention on Human Rights prohibiting inhuman and degrading treatment. The government appealed, and at year's end, the case was pending further review.

According to the Correctional Services Academy, there was one suicide in prison as of June.

Administration: Authorities permitted prisoners and detainees to submit complaints to judicial authorities without censorship and to request investigation of credible allegations of inhuman conditions. As of September authorities were investigating one such allegation but had not reached a conclusion.

Independent Monitoring: The government permitted visits by independent human rights observers, including the Council of Europe's Committee for the Prevention of Torture. Visits occurred throughout the year.

d. Arbitrary Arrest or Detention

The constitution and law prohibit arbitrary arrest and detention, and the government generally observed these prohibitions.

Role of the Police and Security Apparatus

The national police have primary responsibility for internal security. Police may call on the armed forces for assistance in crises. In such circumstances the armed forces operate under police authority. The National Police Directorate oversees the police force.

Civilian authorities maintained effective control over the national police, and the government has effective mechanisms to investigate and punish abuse and corruption. There were no reports of impunity involving the security forces during the year.

Arrest Procedures and Treatment of Detainees

The law requires warrants authorized by a prosecutor for arrests. If police arrest a person without prior authorization, a prosecutor must consider as soon as possible whether the detention should be upheld. Detainees must be informed of the charges against them within three days after their arrest. A prosecutor must arraign arrested suspects no later than three days after arrest. The arraigning judge determines whether the accused should be held in custody or released pending trial. There is no bail system. Officials routinely released defendants accused of minor crimes pending trial, including nonresident foreigners. Defendants accused of serious or violent crimes usually remained in custody until trial. Before interrogation, authorities allowed arrested persons access to a lawyer of their choice or to an attorney appointed by the government. The government pays the attorney fees in all cases. Authorities usually allowed arrested persons access to family members.

The law mandates that detainees be transferred from a temporary police holding cell to a regular prison cell within 48 hours. Authorities did not always observe this time limit.

The law provides that a court must supervise whether and how long a detainee may be held in solitary confinement during pretrial detention, but a regulation provides exemptions in cases of insufficient space due to building conditions, such as construction work, or inadequate staffing. Although the Ministry of Justice and Public Security did not keep statistics on the use of this exemption, since 2012 prison authorities performed 11 spot counts of prisoners in solitary confinement.

Detainee's Ability to Challenge Lawfulness of Detention before a Court: Persons arrested or detained are entitled to challenge in court the legal basis of their detention and obtain prompt release and compensation if found to have been unlawfully detained.

e. Denial of Fair Public Trial

The constitution and law provide for an independent judiciary, and the government generally respected judicial independence.

Trial Procedures

The constitution and the law provide for the right to a fair public trial, and an independent judiciary generally enforced this right. Defendants enjoy a presumption of innocence and the right to be informed promptly and in detail of the charges against them. They have access to free interpretation as necessary from the moment charged through all appeals. Trials are fair and public and held without undue delay. Defendants have the right to be present at their trials. Defendants also have the right to counsel at public expense, to have adequate time and facilities to prepare a defense, to have access to government-held evidence, to confront and question adverse witnesses, to present their own evidence and witnesses, and to appeal. Defendants may not be compelled to testify or to confess guilt. The law extends these rights to all defendants.

Political Prisoners and Detainees

There were no reports of political prisoners or detainees.

Civil Judicial Procedures and Remedies

Individuals or organizations may seek civil remedies for human rights violations through domestic courts. They may appeal cases alleging violations of the European Convention on Human Rights by the government to the European Court of Human Rights after they have exhausted all avenues of appeal in domestic courts.

f. Arbitrary or Unlawful Interference with Privacy, Family, Home, or Correspondence

The constitution and law prohibit such actions, and there were no reports that the government failed to respect these prohibitions.

Racial profiling is against the law, but authorities did not keep records relating to stop and search of members of vulnerable groups. NGOs such as the Organization against Public Discrimination reported complaints of police profiling from members of the immigrant population from Africa and the Middle East, particularly the young. According to the groups, many incidents went unreported to authorities because victims declined to pursue charges.

Section 2. Respect for Civil Liberties, Including:

a. Freedom of Speech and Press

The constitution and law provide for freedom of speech and press, and the government generally respected these rights. An independent press, an effective judiciary, and a functioning democratic political system combined to promote freedom of speech and press.

<u>Freedom of Speech and Expression</u>: The law prohibits "threatening or insulting anyone, or inciting hatred or repression of or contempt for anyone because of his or her: a) skin color or national or ethnic origin; b) religion or life stance; c) sexual orientation or lifestyle, or d) disability." Violators are subject to a fine or imprisonment not to exceed three years. According to the ombudsman for equality and discrimination (LDO), hate speech on the internet against ethnic minorities, women, and LGBTI persons was a problem.

In August a court in Fredrikstad convicted a man of malicious hate speech online for a posting on Facebook targeting Muslims. He was sentenced to pay a fine of 12,000 kroner ($1,450) or go to prison for 22 days. The police hate crime unit charged the man with making a physical threat and "promoting hatred and contempt" against a group of Emirati tourists visiting the town.

During the year the NGO Norwegian Center against Racism observed an increase in hateful rhetoric in online commentaries and social media towards politicians with a minority background.

<u>Press and Media Freedoms</u>: The independent media were active and expressed a wide variety of views without restriction. The prohibitions against hate speech also applied to the print and broadcast media, the publication of books, and online newspapers and journals.

Internet Freedom

The government did not restrict or disrupt access to the internet or censor online content, and there were no credible reports that the government monitored private online communications without appropriate legal authority. According to the International Telecommunication Union, 39 percent of the population had a fixed broadband subscription, and 97 percent of the population used the internet.

Academic Freedom and Cultural Events

There were no government restrictions on academic freedom or cultural events.

b. Freedom of Peaceful Assembly and Association

The constitution and law provide for the freedoms of assembly and association, and the government generally respected these rights.

c. Freedom of Religion

See the Department of State's *International Religious Freedom Report* at www.state.gov/religiousfreedomreport/.

d. Freedom of Movement, Internally Displaced Persons, Protection of Refugees, and Stateless Persons

The law provides for freedom of internal movement, foreign travel, emigration, and repatriation, and the government generally respected these rights.

The government cooperated with the Office of the UN High Commissioner for Refugees (UNHCR) and other humanitarian organizations in providing protection and assistance to refugees, asylum seekers, stateless persons, and other persons of concern.

Protection of Refugees

Access to Asylum: The law provides for the granting of asylum or refugee status, and the government has established a system for providing protection to refugees. On June 10, parliament tightened the country's immigration laws to make greater use of biometrics for identification and to impose stricter Norwegian-language requirements for permanent residency.

Through the end of October, a reported 2,804 persons had applied for asylum in the country. In contrast, in 2015 more than 31,000 persons applied for asylum in the country. As of the end of October, more than 17,000 persons were living in asylum reception centers. Many of the asylum claims processed during the year were based on applications submitted in 2015.

The law permits detention of migrants to establish their identity or to affect their removal from the country if authorities deem it likely the persons would evade an order to leave.

Safe Country of Origin/Transit: The country is party to the EU's Dublin III regulation, which allows the government to return asylum seekers to the first country they entered that is also a party to the regulation. As of August the government transferred 1,134 persons to other European countries under the regulation. Authorities did not return asylum seekers to Greece.

Refoulement: Authorities deported failed asylum seekers and others who had no legal right to stay in the country to Russia, Nigeria, Iraq, Somalia, Afghanistan, and other countries. A number of NGOs criticized the government for returning some failed asylum seekers to areas in their home country different from where they originated, as frequently occurred for returnees to Afghanistan.

Freedom of Movement: Asylum seekers residing in an asylum reception center may not be absent from the center for more than three days without potentially losing their place at the center and all concomitant financial support from the government. Centers were often located in remote areas of the country, and long travel times and a lack of money to pay for public transport effectively limited asylum seekers' ability to move freely. Residents may apply for permission to live away from the reception center temporarily. Migrants who do not qualify for asylum are generally permitted to remain in asylum centers while awaiting voluntary return, assisted return, or forced return.

Employment: Asylum seekers may not work while their cases are under evaluation unless their identity can be documented through a valid travel document or a national identification card. Those who do not possess a work permit or other legal status are generally not permitted to work.

Durable Solutions: The government's Directorate of Immigration (UDI) had several programs to settle refugees permanently in the country. According to the UDI, as of August the country had accepted 2,478 refugees for resettlement. Through the International Organization for Migration and other government partners, the government assisted the return of unsuccessful asylum seekers to their country of origin through voluntary programs that offered financial and logistical support for repatriation. Identity documents issued by either the Norwegian or the returnee's government are required in order to use this program. The government continued routinely to offer migrants 20,000 kroner ($2,410) in addition to airfare to encourage persons with weak asylum claims to leave the country.

<u>Temporary Protection</u>: Through the end of August, the government provided temporary protection to 224 individuals who may not qualify as refugees.

Stateless Persons

According to UNHCR statistics, there were 2,561 stateless persons in the country as of January; they were not counted as refugees. According to the UDI, at the end of August, an additional 811 stateless asylum seekers lived in receiving centers, a decrease of 7 percent from the same period in 2015. Of these, 254 persons had permission to stay, and 116 were under orders to leave the country. The remainder continued the asylum application process.

Citizenship is derived from one's parents, and children born in the country do not automatically become citizens. The government effectively implemented laws and policies to provide stateless persons the opportunity to gain nationality on a nondiscriminatory basis.

Section 3. Freedom to Participate in the Political Process

The constitution and law provide citizens the ability to choose their government in free and fair periodic elections held by secret ballot and based on universal and equal suffrage.

Elections and Political Participation

<u>Recent Elections</u>: Observers considered the parliamentary elections held in 2013 to be free and fair.

<u>Participation of Women and Minorities</u>: No laws limit the participation of women and members of minorities in the political process, and women and minorities did so.

Section 4. Corruption and Lack of Transparency in Government

The law provides criminal penalties for corruption by officials, and the government generally implemented the law effectively. There were no reports of government or police corruption.

Financial Disclosure: By law income and asset information from the tax forms of all citizens, including public officials, must be made public each year. Failure to declare properly may result in up to two years in prison. Each year officials must declare income, assets, liabilities, and holdings in public companies.

Public Access to Information: The law provides for public access to nearly all government information except for classified national security information, and the government provided access to both citizens and noncitizens, including foreign media. The government generally provided information in a timely manner.

Section 5. Governmental Attitude Regarding International and Nongovernmental Investigation of Alleged Violations of Human Rights

A variety of domestic and international human rights groups generally operated without government restriction, investigating and publishing their findings on human rights cases. Government officials often were cooperative and responsive to their views.

Government Human Rights Bodies: The country has ombudsmen for public administration, children, and equality and antidiscrimination. The ombudsman for public administration is appointed by parliament, while the government appoints the others. All ombudsmen were adequately resourced, enjoyed the government's cooperation, and operated without government interference. The ombudsmen for public administration and for equality and antidiscrimination hear complaints against actions by government officials. Although the ombudsmen's recommendations are not legally binding, authorities usually complied with them.

Parliament's Standing Committee on Scrutiny and Constitutional Affairs reviews the reports of the public administration ombudsmen, while its Standing Committee on Justice is responsible for matters relating to the judicial system, police, and the penal, civil, and criminal codes.

The National Institution for Human Rights reports directly to parliament on the human rights situation in the country. It makes recommendations to help ensure that the country's international human rights obligations are fulfilled by advising the government, disseminating information, promoting education and research on human rights, and facilitating cooperation with relevant public bodies. The organization submits an annual report on human rights in the country.

Section 6. Discrimination, Societal Abuses, and Trafficking in Persons

Women

Rape and Domestic Violence: The law criminalizes rape, including spousal rape, and the government generally enforced the law. The penalty for rape is two to 21 years in prison, depending on the severity of the assault, the age of the victim, and the circumstances in which the crime occurred. Very few cases resulted in a sentence longer than three years and four months in prison.

Amnesty International Norway continued to claim that the law inadequately protected women against violence and that statistics on rape and sexual assault were not regularly updated. Amnesty criticized police for poor investigation of rape cases and cited a lack of training for lay judges, resulting in personal prejudices affecting the judges' vote. Media reports of transcripts and discussions among lay judges in several rape cases showed prejudices regarding the victim's skirt length, the amount of alcohol consumed prior to the rape, and statements such as "that slut was looking for it wearing a dress like that."

Violence against women, including spousal abuse, was a problem. The law provides higher penalties for domestic violence (one to three years in prison) than for simple assault, with an increased term of up to six years in more severe cases and up to 21 years for aggravated rape. The government generally enforced the law, although the foundation Oslo Crisis Center continued to criticize the conviction rate (approximately 10 percent) as too low.

The government had programs to prevent rape and domestic violence and to counsel victims. Following the consolidation of police districts from 27 to 12 as of January 1, all 12 districts had a domestic violence coordinator.

Public and private organizations operated 45 government-funded shelters and managed five 24-hour crisis hotlines. The Oslo Crisis Center believed that the network of shelters was too small and that many women were less likely or unable to seek help, since they would have to travel long distances to do so, especially in the sparsely populated districts in the north of the country. The shelters provided support and counseling for victims and helped them gain access to social services, doctors, lawyers, and housing authorities. Survivors of domestic violence have a right to consult a lawyer free of charge before deciding whether to make a formal complaint. If the government initiates criminal proceedings, the survivor is entitled to free assistance from a victim's advocate.

Sexual Harassment: The law provides that "employees shall not be subjected to harassment or other unseemly behavior," and the government effectively enforced this provision. Employers who violate this law are subject to fines or prison sentences of up to two years, depending on the seriousness of the offense. The ombudsman for equality and antidiscrimination concluded that sexual harassment was not an acute problem in the country.

Reproductive Rights: Couples and individuals have the right to decide the number, spacing, and timing of their children; manage their reproductive health; and have access to the information and means to do so, free from discrimination, coercion, or violence.

Discrimination: Women have the same legal status as men. Approximately 28 percent, or 50 of the 181 complaints received and investigated by the ombudsman for equality and antidiscrimination in 2015, concerned discrimination based on gender. Women experienced discrimination in employment.

The law mandates that 40 percent of the members of boards of directors of publicly listed companies be women, and virtually all public companies complied with the law.

Children

Birth Registration: Citizenship is derived from one's parents; children born in the country do not automatically become citizens. All birth clinics in the country reported births to a central birth register and provided the parents with a birth certificate. The birth certificate does not confer citizenship.

Child Abuse: During the year the government amended the law to include sexual offenses against children under the age of 14 under the definition of rape. In 2015 the Norwegian Directorate for Children, Youth, and Family Affairs initiated 43,681 investigations of alleged child abuse and completed 44,100. By the end of 2015, approximately 36,800 children had received assistance from the Child Welfare Services, of whom 21,950 received in-home assistance, while 14,850 were removed from their family home.

An independent children's ombudsman office within the Ministry of Children, Equality, and Social Inclusion is responsible under the law for the protection of children and providing assistance and support services. With five regional offices and 26 professional teams, the office is the government's principal agency for the welfare and protection of children and families. If criminal proceedings are initiated, the victim is entitled to free assistance from a victim's advocate.

Early and Forced Marriage: The minimum legal age for marriage in the country is 18 for both women and men, although a 16-year-old child may marry with the consent of parents or guardians and permission from the county governor. The county governor may give permission only when there are "special reasons for contracting a marriage."

Sexual Exploitation of Children: Commercial sexual exploitation of children under the age of 18 is illegal, both in the country and when committed abroad by a citizen of the country. In both cases the punishment is either a fine or a prison sentence of up to two years. Child pornography is also illegal and punishable by a fine or a prison sentence of up to three years. The government generally enforced the laws. The age for consensual sex is 16.

International Child Abductions: The country is a party to the 1980 Hague Convention on the Civil Aspects of International Child Abduction. See the Department of State's *Annual Report on International Parental Child Abduction* at travel.state.gov/content/childabduction/en/legal/compliance.html.

Anti-Semitism

There were approximately 1,500-2,000 Jews in the country, 747 of whom belonged to Jewish congregations. Jewish Community leaders reported the public generally supported the community.

Anti-Semitism was bundled with other hate crimes in the country's statistics. Police stated that the number of anti-Semitism cases was too low to warrant a separate reporting mechanism.

On October 2, the government released an 11-point action plan to counter anti-Semitism in society. The plan emphasized training and education programs, research on anti-Semitism and Jewish life in the country, and efforts to safeguard the country's Jewish culture. It also adopted anti-Semitism as a separate category of hate crime in police statistics.

Trafficking in Persons

See the Department of State's *Trafficking in Persons Report* at
www.state.gov/j/tip/rls/tiprpt/.

Persons with Disabilities

The constitution and law prohibit discrimination against persons with disabilities in
employment, education, air travel and other transportation, access to health care,
the judicial system, and the provision of other governmental services, and the
government effectively implemented and enforced these provisions. The law
applies to all persons with disabilities without enumerating specific types of
disabilities. It mandates access to public buildings, information, and
communications for persons with disabilities. The most common problem reported
by the LDO was access for persons with physical disabilities (60 such complaints
in 2015), such as lack of ramps for wheelchair users where there are steps or stairs
to enter a building. In 2009 the government began implementing the Norway
Universally Designed by 2025 action plan, which works to ensure increased
accessibility for persons with disabilities.

National/Racial/Ethnic Minorities

Discrimination against immigrants, including asylum seekers and irregular
migrants, and ethnic minorities remained a problem. Ethnic discrimination
occurred in employment.

A review by the UN Committee on the Elimination of Racial Discrimination
released in 2015 stated that authorities did not fully address problems such as
racism and hate speech. Although the law prohibits discrimination based on
ethnicity, the committee specifically identified the law's omission of race as a
prohibited basis of discrimination, the government's lack of statistical information
about the ethnic composition and well-being of the population, and "the increase in
hate speech and xenophobic discourse by politicians and in media and other public
platforms, including via internet."

The Norwegian Center against Racism continued its criticism of the government
for lacking an action plan against racism.

Indigenous People

Although there is no official registry of Sami in the country, as of January 2015, approximately 55,600 persons were estimated to live north of Saltfjellet, an area in northern Norway with a significant Sami majority. In addition to participating freely in the national political process, the Sami elect their own parliament, the Samediggi. The law establishing the Sami parliament stipulates that the 39-seat consultative group meet regularly to deal with "all matters, which in [its] opinion are of special importance to the Sami people."

On August 9, the UN special rapporteur on the rights of indigenous persons noted problems of unclear and unsecure Sami land and resource rights outside Finnmark County and of instances where respect was not paid to the customs, traditions, and land tenure systems of the Sami people.

Noting that sea salmon fishing and spring duck hunting in the municipality of Guovdageaidnu/Kautokeino form an important part of Sami cultural heritage, the special rapporteur stated there were insufficient safeguards on sea salmon fishing and spring duck hunting to ensure they could be pursued and maintained according to Sami tradition in a culturally and ecologically sustainable way. The special rapporteur identified a need to ensure that the mining law requires adequate consultations with the affected indigenous communities.

Sami officials continued to report that authorities did not provide sufficient access to Sami language resources.

In addition to the Sami, five ethnically non-Norwegian groups with a long-standing attachment to the country have a special protected status under the law: Kvens/Norwegian Finns (people of Finnish descent in Northern Norway), Jews, Forest Finns, Roma, and Romani/Tater people (a distinct group of travelers who emigrated to Norway and Sweden in the 1500s).

Acts of Violence, Discrimination, and Other Abuses Based on Sexual Orientation and Gender Identity

The law prohibits discrimination based on sexual orientation and gender identity. While violence motivated by discriminatory attitudes towards transgender persons is not considered a hate crime, crimes based on discriminatory attitudes towards sexual orientation can be treated as aggravated crimes.

The NGO Association for Gender and Sexual Diversity (previously known as the LLH) estimated that a significant number of crimes against LGBTI individuals were not reported to police. One police station in Oslo, Manglerud, had a dedicated task force to work on hate crimes and reported 30 registered cases of hate crimes towards the LGBTI community during the year through September. There were 33 such cases reported in 2015.

The LGBTI community experienced a rise in online harassment from a neo-Nazi group that photographed the pride parades in Oslo and Kristiansand and then posted the images online with derogatory captions. In Kristiansand the group also removed rainbow flags from flagpoles, burned them, and posted the images online.

Transgender persons may administratively change their name. On May 30, parliament approved legislation to allow persons who are 16 and older (and from age 6 to 16 with parental permission) to change their gender on legal identification documents based on gender identity without having to undergo surgery or physical transformation. Previously, a person had to be diagnosed as having a "transsexual gender identity disorder" and undergo a sex-change operation, a process that could take as long as 10 years.

Other Societal Violence or Discrimination

The Norwegian Center against Racism reported continued anti-Muslim and anti-Arab sentiment in society. The Muslim community asserted that its complaints were ignored in public debate.

Section 7. Worker Rights

a. Freedom of Association and the Right to Collective Bargaining

The law provides for the right of workers, including migrant workers (those who have a work permit in the country), to form and join independent unions, bargain collectively, and conduct legal strikes. The government generally respected these rights. The law prohibits antiunion discrimination and requires reinstatement of workers fired for union activity.

The right to strike excludes members of the military and senior civil servants. With the approval of parliament, the government may compel arbitration in any industrial sector if it is determined that a strike threatens public safety. Trade unions criticized the government for intervening too quickly in labor disputes, although the law generally allows unions to conduct their activities without government interference.

The government effectively enforced applicable laws. Resources and remediation efforts were adequate. Penalties for violations in the form of fines are set by the labor court and vary according to the magnitude of damage, the injuring party's guilt and financial sustainability, the injured party's circumstances, and the conditions in general.

When an employer violates labor statutes or regulations, the Norwegian Labor Inspection Authority (NLIA), which is part of the Ministry of Labor and Social Affairs, may order the employer in writing to correct the situation within a specified time limit. The employer may file an appeal. If the employer fails to comply, the NLIA may impose fines or close the employer's enterprise. The penalties were sufficient to deter violations.

The government and employers respected freedom of association and the right to collective bargaining. Employers and unions participated in collective bargaining during the year.

b. Prohibition of Forced or Compulsory Labor

The law prohibits all forms of forced or compulsory labor, and the government effectively enforced laws against it. A maximum sentence of 10 years' imprisonment for violations of the law was sufficiently stringent to deter violations. When the NLIA determines that an employer has violated these laws, it refers the case to police. As of August police received 69 reports of forced labor from the NLIA.

Traffickers subjected men and women, mostly migrants, to forced labor in the domestic service, nursing, and construction sectors. Forced labor and trafficking discussions in the country generally focus on prostitutes, seen as a large victim group. The government doubled state funds available to NGOs working with trafficking problems in 2015, which led to new initiatives related to assisting victims of forced labor. During the height of the influx of asylum seekers and irregular migrants in late 2015 and early 2016, there was extensive media reporting on unaccompanied minor asylum seekers who "disappeared" from asylum reception centers and were feared to be victims of trafficking and forced labor. During the year the same concerns applied to those who disappeared from asylum centers after receiving a final rejection of their claims. Children were subjected to forced labor (see section 7.c.).

Also see the Department of State's *Trafficking in Persons Report* at www.state.gov/j/tip/rls/tiprpt/.

c. Prohibition of Child Labor and Minimum Age for Employment

Children between the ages of 13 and 15 may be employed up to 12 hours per week in light work that does not adversely affect their health, development, or schooling. Examples of light work include assistant work in offices or stores. Children under age 15 need parental permission to work and those older than 15 can work as part of vocational training, as long as they are supervised. Between the ages of 15 and 18, children not in school may work up to 40 hours per week and a maximum eight hours per day. For children who remain in school, the law limits work to only those hours "not affecting schooling" without specific limits, but less than 40 hours per week. No child may work at night between the hours of 9 p.m. and 6 a.m. Working more than nine hours a week qualifies a child for health benefits.

The government enforced the laws on child labor effectively. Penalties include an unspecified fine, imprisonment of up two years, or both. The penalties were sufficient to deter violations. NLIA resources were adequate to enforce the law effectively.

While employers generally observed minimum age rules, there were reports that children were trafficked for forced labor. Children were subjected to forced begging and criminal activity, particularly drug smuggling and theft. Commercial sexual exploitation of children also occurred. There were also reports of children forced to work as unpaid domestic help.

d. Discrimination with Respect to Employment and Occupation

Labor laws and regulations prohibit discrimination in employment and occupation based on race, ethnicity, color, sex, religion, political opinion, national origin, social origin or status, disability, sexual orientation or gender identity, age, language, or HIV-positive status or having other communicable diseases. The government effectively enforced these laws and regulations. Victims of discrimination can claim in the courts redress and compensation covering financial loss associated with the discrimination. The penalties were sufficient to deter violations. The LDO received 181 complaints of discrimination in 2015, a 15 percent decrease from the year before.

Discrimination in employment and occupation occurred with respect to gender and ethnicity. Discrimination against Romani and migrant workers also occurred.

The law provides that women and men engaged in the same activity shall receive equal wages for work of equal value. In 2015 women earned on average 13.9 percent less than men on a monthly basis, according to the Statistics Bureau. The government attributed this to differences in the professions chosen by women and men and the predominance of women in part-time or public sector work. The ombudsman for equality and antidiscrimination expressed concern that many women were in part-time positions involuntarily because of a tendency in certain industries, such as health and services, to divide work into a large number of part-time positions with no meaningful opportunity for full-time employment. According to the Statistics Bureau, in the third quarter of the year, nearly 37 percent of women and 15 percent of men worked part time.

Equally qualified immigrants sometimes had more difficulty finding employment than ethnic Norwegians. As of June the unemployment rate among immigrants was 7 percent, compared with 2.1 percent among nonimmigrants, according to government statistics. African immigrants had the highest unemployment rate at 11.2 percent, followed by immigrants from eastern EU countries at 8.4 percent, South and Central Americans at 7.9 percent, and Asians at 7.5 percent.

e. Acceptable Conditions of Work

The law does not mandate an official minimum wage. Instead, minimum wages were set in collective bargaining agreements. Statistics Norway uses 60 percent of the median income for the relative poverty limit, which was 207,400 kroner per year in 2014 for a single person ($25,000).

The law limits the normal workweek to 37.5 hours and provides for 25 working days of paid leave per year (31 days for workers over the age of 60). The law mandates a 28-hour rest period on weekends and holidays. The law provides for premium pay of 40 percent of salary for overtime and prohibits compulsory overtime in excess of 10 hours per week.

The law provides the same benefits for citizens and foreign workers with residency permits but forbids the employment of foreign workers who do not have residency permits. The law provides for safe and physically acceptable working conditions for all employed persons. The NLIA, in consultation with nongovernment experts, sets occupational safety and health standards. The law requires enterprises with 50 or more workers to establish environment committees composed of management, workers, and health-care personnel. Enterprises with 10 or more workers must have safety delegates elected by their employees. Workers may remove themselves from situations that endanger health or safety without jeopardy to their employment; authorities effectively protected employees in this situation.

The NLIA effectively enforced laws and standards regarding acceptable work conditions in the formal sector. The NLIA had 630 employees, 350 of whom were labor inspectors; the number of labor inspectors was sufficient to enforce compliance. The NLIA may close an enterprise immediately if the life or health of employees is in imminent danger and may report enterprises to police for serious breaches of the law. A serious violation may result in fines or, in the worst case, imprisonment. The penalties were sufficient to deter violations. The government's Working Environment Act, last amended in December 2015, addresses labor market problems in the country.

Some employers in the cleaning, hotel, domestic service, construction, and transport industries (some of which was in the informal sector) underpaid foreign workers and subjected them to working hours beyond legally permissible limits. These sectors were a priority for labor inspection by the NLIA in the *Strategic Plan for Labor Inspection (2013-2016)*.

www.ingramcontent.com/pod-product-compliance
Lightning Source LLC
Chambersburg PA
CBHW080822280726

48660CB00018B/3566